Haikus, Haikus and more Haikus

– ASHOK SAWHNY –

An environmentally friendly book printed and bound in England by
www.printondemand-worldwide.com

This book is made entirely of chain-of-custody materials

www.fast-print.net/store.php

HAIKUS, HAIKUS AND MORE HAIKUS

A catalogue record for this book is available from the British Library

ISBN 978-178456-240-3

First published 2015 by
FASTPRINT PUBLISHING
Peterborough, England.

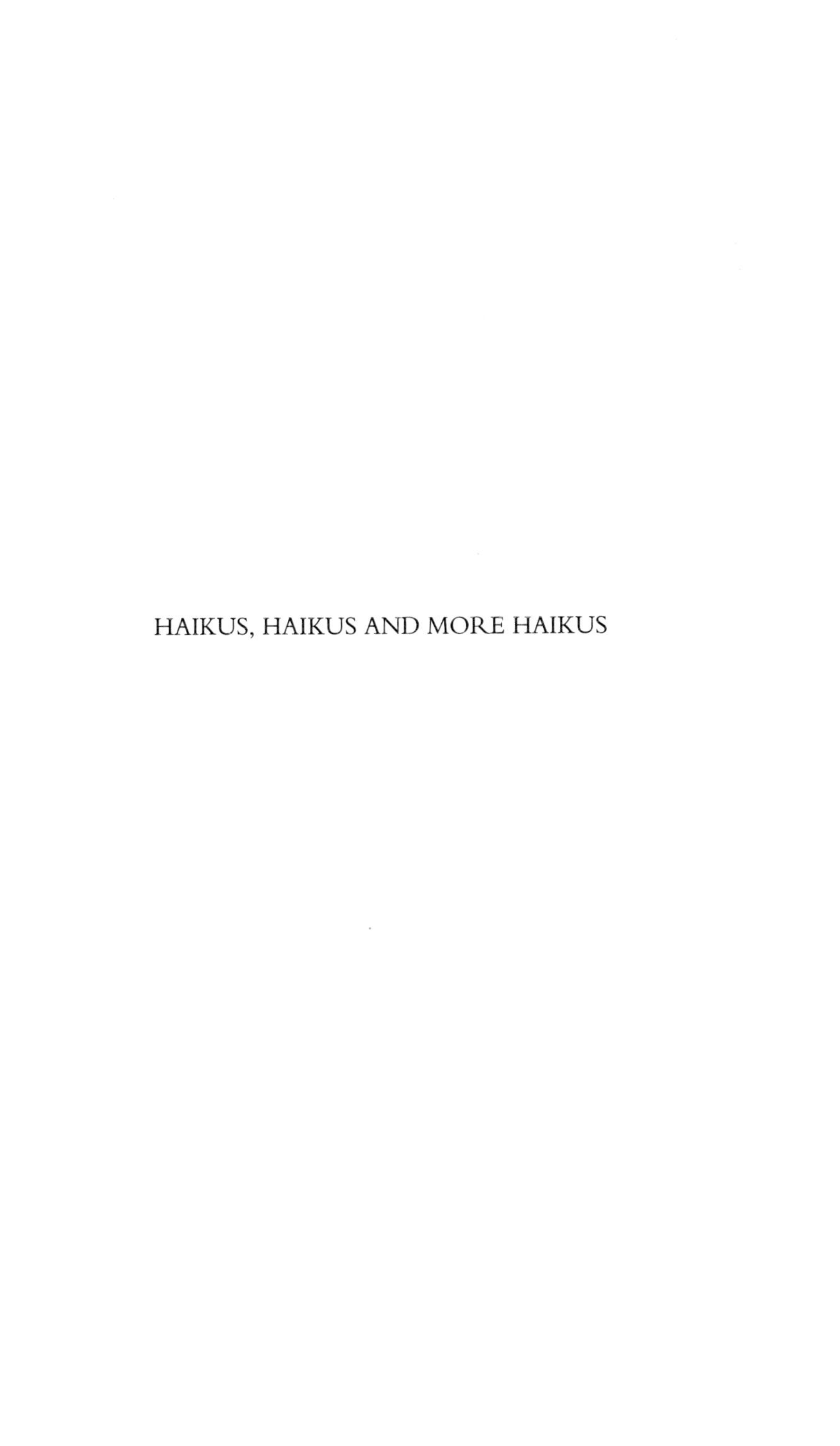

HAIKUS, HAIKUS AND MORE HAIKUS

1. O, Chrysanthemum,
You are more than just a flower,
A nation's lost Hope.

2. Cherry Blossoms are
The awakening of Spring,
From a harsh winter's sleep.

3. A blanket of clouds,
Enwraps me and Mother Earth,
How complete, Nature,

4. We call them rain drops,
These lovely showers from heaven,
Are they someone' tears?

5. Walking in the rain,
So purifying, so fresh,
The end of summer's pain,

6. I love this breeze,
A little wet from the rain,
Or cool if you please.

7. Rain turns to ice drops,
And snowflakes cover the ground,
A pretty picture.

8. Tall, dark, handsome, fair
A man here, a woman there,
Romance in the air.

9. Snow on the mountains,
Winter's around the corner,
There's cold in my bones.

10. A lilt in my heart,
A hop, a skip and a jump,
And Spring in my arms.

11. The sweat of my brow,
Does the summer's story tell
Golly, hot and how!

12. And then comes Autumn,
And the cycle is complete,
With seasons in verse.

13. When night falls it's dark,
And your'e scared cos you can't see,
Isn't god in your park?

14. When I am mortal
What for me is forever ?
And who eternal?

15. Lonely seem the stars,
In a very crowded sky,
Heart- rending their cry,

16. Tears from the heavens,
In the form of a cloud burst,
And we think it's rain,

17. How silly we are !
How little we understand !
Of another's pain,

18. If other's pain hurts
Insensate we shall not be,
And will offer balm.

19. In the aftermath
Of war lies peace in tatters,
Does anyone care?

20. Guns & roses are
A strange combination, but,
So is war & peace!

21. How still lies the sea,
Like the lull before the storm,
O, how heavenly!

22. O, for clear blue skies
And rays that don't hurt the eyes
Is that asking much?

23. When your smile is bright
Then why do the eyes look sad?
Is your heart not glad?

24. Life a mystery
A conundrum, that we live,
And then simply, die.

25. Always, Eternal,
Empty words, forever said,
Where is my Conscience.

26. A world of untruths
How many lies can they tell,
Purveyors of Peace.

27. In the aftermath
Of storms, typhoons and tempests,
Does Life bestow calm.

28. The allure of heights,
The mountain top and skies blue,
Will I ever rue?

29. She passed me by, and
As she did I saw a tear,
Was it joy or fear ?

30. The lines on my hand,
Reveal the lie of the land,
Like footprints on sand.

31. Church, temple mosque , all divine,
Then why must man, man malign?
Dear God, aren't we thine?

32. All your power and pelf,
Will leave you just where you are,
When Time comes calling.

33. Teardrops from heaven,
Those who've left me are with Him,
Wonder who's crying ?

34. Moods are like breezes,
Look at typhoons and tempests,
Zephyrs and freezes.

35. With myself do I speak,
How empty are those who others' seek,
For I am my world.

36. O, those drifting leaves,
And butterflies in the breeze,
How light they must be !

37. Lust, greed , ambition,
Three pillars of destruction,
Oh, what Temptation!

38. Life so transparent,
If you don't hide behind lies,
Then Truth you can see.

39. I hear a child's cry,
Mother, tell me where am I?
Alone without you.

40. To the light of day,
And to sleep at night, do I
Not have equal right ?

41. The clouds are dark, but,
Where is that silver lining?
And where the lone star ?

42. How light the burden
Of the tree that's laden with fruit,
How joyful reward !

43. Silence is golden
For who ever heard God speak,
So hold your peace, friends.

44. No greater magic,
Was ever created than
Mystery of Man,

45. When a heart sings true,
What use to me, melody?
Or stars in the sky.

46. Like the mellow sun
On a face that does love show,
There is warmth and glow.

47. Green grass on the hill,
The littlest of things can thrill,
Simple life, no frill

48. Will my paths be strewn
With rose petals all the way,
Who knows , who can say?

49. You can't buy silence,
How priceless a tranquil mind,
O, worthless money!

50. Never hurt a fly,
Cos they can take grievances,
Straight up to the sky

51. Time ripens the seed,
And age to wisdom does the same,
How ephemeral is fame.

52. If there were no thorns,
Roses might not have been there,
Life is not all flowers.

53. The eyes never lie,
For they just mirror the soul,
And that's where Truth lies.

54. Manage your temper,
Hold your horses and calm down,
Canter, don't gallop.

55. It saves us from cold,
Why is summer under fire?
Let's happily perspire!

56. If the trees are bare,
Does it mean winters' around,
Or is mankind there?

57. Snow melts, rivers flow
Down mountainsides to the sea,
Their own Destiny.

58. I asked you to dance
And you readily agreed,
I'm in a trance.

59. The warmth of a smile,
The beauty of innocence,
Unpretentious guile.

60. The ocean's floor
Has riches beyond compare,
Gems serene and more.

61. At one's mothers feet
Lies the stairway to heaven,
And eternal peace.

62. Tell me what's excess,
Beyond means or desire,
Ambition or greed?

63. Straw by straw by straw,
Ever seen a sparrows nest?
Patience put to test.

64. Why are thoughts so wild,
Like scampering squirrels all,
Up and down mind's wall

65. If Spring were a flower,
Would winter be the dark hour
Autumn red and gold,

66. If whirlwinds you reap,
What did you sow pray tell me?
Promises not keep?

67. We freeze in the cold,
And yet the heart is warmed by
Whisky and ice cube.

68. If clouds have linings
Silver or gold, whatever,
Where are my rainbows?

69. No greater triumph,
Than mastery over self
For then you're with Him.

70. See a seed sprouting,
Then blossoming as a bud,
That is life and death

71. The seed asks for rain.
With faith in the Almighty.
And so it receives.

72. They call it lightning,
A bolt from the blue hit me,
I thought it was Truth.

73. Petal by petal,
Does the flower finally form,
And that's how it dies.

74. The lotus flower has
A unique story to tell,
Beauty lies within.

75. Storms ravage the shore
And then spent retreat to base,
Orgasmic ally.

76. As with ponds and lakes
The minds like muddied water.
Till it settles down.

77. Waves are like desire,
Which too retreat to return,
When thirst is whetted.

78. Nothing 's really mine,
What I don't own I can't lose,
Is loss notional ?

79. Red and gold make brown,
Black and white makes it all grey,
What is ever plain?

80. Spontaneity,
Do what you must here and now,
With adequate care

81. What is a paradox?
That which is one thing and then,
Maybe another.

82. Brain power, grey matter,
Use it while you have it, for
You could then lose it.

83. I think I'm clever,
But that's not what matters cos,
It's for you to judge.

84. How big is your world?
You, your family, you friends,
That's it and no more.

85. What is heavenly?
The scent of a woman or
The joy of the cup.

86. The essence of life
Is to live it happily,
And that you define.

87. What is forever?
Who wants to live forever,
One life is enough.

88. When it rains it's tears,
When there are blossoms it's smiles,
Why fight with Nature?

89. It's nice to be nice
But it's nicer to be true,
Even when it hurts.

90. Let's eat some rice then
Run around the park but thrice,
And then pay the price!!

91. What's Profundity?
Understanding things simply,
You need no Plato!

92. What keeps me alive?
The coursing blood through my veins,
And the will of God!

93. It will nag and neigh
Try calling the horse, donkey,
Let's go ask the Bard.

94. A moment of time,
The microcosm of life,
What do you wait for?

95. My mind is gloomy
And dawn is a long way off,
What will my stars do?

96. No frowns, no creases,
Is happiness just a smile?
Pause, stop, think a while.

97. I saw a squirrel
Go nutty with a walnut,
How corny is life!

98. Watch a river flow,
Then see your own emotions,
How close the ripples.

99. I am happy on earth,
What will I do with the skies?
That's another world.

100. An ant is tireless,
A worker in it's own right,
Small is beautiful.

101. Why don't we relax?
Slow and steady wins the race,
Then why force the pace.

102. There is no light found,
When the soul is in darkness,
And Satan's around.

103. The soaring eagles,
Arouse adventure in me,
Wish I too could fly.

104. O, my cup of tea,
Wake me up and set me free,
From the chains of night.

105. Where is Paradise?
Does heaven lie in the skies?
Hallucination.

106. If Self is selfish,
What must I do please tell me,
To neglect myself.

107. The passage of time,
Is only me growing old,
Who else, who else, who?

108. We all live our lives,
History is my story,
How does it help you?

109. Renunciation,
Will that bring me peace of mind?
Or is that escape?

110. Tell me is love just
A chemical reaction,
Is that all it is?

111. Yesterday 'twas me
I told the sky I was sad,
Now the sky is sad.

112. The earth looked so parched,
I wished to be a cloud to
Quench and slake its thirst.

113. A broken heart is like,
Ashes immersed in tears,
And a withered flower.

114. Life's hazy, Obscure,
Like a bend in the river,
So go with the flow.

115. The pale silvery moon,
Waves lapping against the shore,
Tranquility reigns.

116. Gurgling in gaiety,
Across the verdant meadows,
The stream meanders.

117. Pink cheeks , lovely smile,
My baby gurgling with joy,
Sets my heart alight.

118. Regal in its flight
Casting a shadow below.
The eagle soars high.

119. High up in the sky.
The kite weaving in and out.
Joyous to behold.

120. The placid blue seas.
The sparkling dew on green grass.
Soothing to tired eyes.

121. Clusters of flowers
The boughs carry the weight well.
Proudly, yet humbly.

122. Circling round the trunk.
The creeper reaches the top.
To bask in the sun.

123. Yellow and gold flecked
The leaves during autumn fall.
New ones take their place.

124. All life was seed once,
Struggling to sprout and to grow
Life must be cherished.

125. Bright red in the sky
The sun on the horizon
The moon waits it's turn.

126. With rain comes rainbow,
Not just sadness, joy as well,
Like day follows night.

127. A joy to behold,
The colours of the rainbow.
Take my breath away

128. The blue skies above
Can thunder and frown as well,
Like my beloved.

129. The life giving sun,
In all its glory and might,
Envies the cool moon.

130. The white fleecy cloud,
Can frown and growl with thunder,
And shed rain like tears.

131. Nature, the teacher,
Imparts important lessons,
Just watch and listen.

132. A hot cup of tea,
Chases the dark blues away,
And lightens the mood.

132. I bow before God,
Allah , Vishnu, God, Rab,
Does the name matter?

133. Life offers you choice
It's then up to you to choose
It's all in your hands.

134. The Sun and the clouds
Play hide and seek and have fun,
Are shadows my fate!

135. If God would be me,
He'd know what He means to me,
Nothing without Him.

136. Life is a bubble,
Beautiful and colourful,
But just as fragile.

137. The dark sky at night ,
Waits to be lit by the sun,
Harbinger of dawn.

138. Galloping horses,
Even they have to slow down,
Just as all life goes.

139. Life offers you much,
You have to take or reject,
It's all in your hands.

140. Flowers give sweet nectar,
Bees help them to propagate,
It's a fair exchange,

141. The morning light thrills,
But the brighter noon does not.,
Moderate is good,

142. Rain pouring in sheets,
Cleanses cities, roads and streets,
Manna to the fields,

143. The overcast sky,
Harbinger of shade and peace,
I find depressing,

144. The wind blows gently,
The sea is calm and peaceful,
Why does my heart yearn?

145. Why is it my wish,
To live life over again,
What would I want changed?

146. Life is but a dream,
Colourful and beautiful,
Who wants to wake up?

147. The setting sun is
Hand clasp of the sea and sky.
And then they let go

148. The smooth gentle waves,
Can turn into tsunamis,
Appearances lie.

149. Shylock was punished,
For demanding interest ,
Which of us does not?

150. Footprints on the sand,
Are they coming or going?
Where to and from where?

151. I want to be lost,
Somewhere where I can't be found,
And be one with God.

152. Do build sand castles,
But they can be washed away ,
So much can go wrong .

153. Stairways to the sky,
Ascend them to reach places,
Don't forget the stairs.

154. The Patter of rain,
The Earth looking washed and clean,
All's right with the world,

155. The Child, an angel,
Innocent and cherubic,
Sign of the future.

156. The cooing pigeons,
Speak of want and tenderness,
Symbols of passion.

157. The scavenger crow,
Cleans the earth of so much debris ,
Serving a purpose,

158. The snow melts and flows,
In the form of streams and brooks,
And preserves nature.

159. The dark of the night,
Time to reflect and think,
Day, the time to act.

160. Man is an actor,
Changing as the need dictates,
Unfair to himself.

161. The deep sea diver,
Brings treasures from the sea bed,
For us to behold.

162. I walk past temples,
Cos I do not need idols,
For He is with me.

163. Soothing to the eyes,
The green of leaves and grass.
Also the blue sky.

164. Cakes, pies and puddings
Are the better things in life,
But not always good.

165. My God within me,
Makes me into a temple
In which He resides.

166. A hand in darkness,
Is what friends are all about,
Clasp the hand warmly.

167. Choose your words with care,
They can shape your destiny,
Words can make or mar.

168. It was all over,
The silence was deafening,
The music faded.

169. My heart heaves a sigh.
Which is really surprising.
We have yet to part.

170. Nothing's wrong with me,
It is the world around
Which is not all right.

171. Might is might, not right,
The weakest can be right too,
And the mighty, Wrong.

172. Cloudy or sunny,
Each morning is a blessing,
Harbinger of life.

173. If I am trusted
I feel more vulnerable,
Than when I am loved.

174. A stream flows forward,
Never back to where it starts,
Life, too, is a stream !

175. Think about life.
Could it have been like a film?
Easy to rewind!

176. I have lived in vain,
For my head is full of me,
And there's more to Life.

177. Your cup overflows,
But don't drink from the saucer,
Share it with others.

178. Give all that you can,
For in giving we receive,
Our good Lord's blessings.

179. Reached out with both hands,
To help those who are in need,
There's joy in giving.

180. I reached for the stars,
Even if I can't touch them,
At least I aspire.

181. People are equal,
We should appreciate, not
Take them for granted.

182. Stardust in my eyes,
Makes the world a better place,
Easier to live.

183. Two divergent paths.
One known, the other unknown,
Which should I take ?

184. Cherries and blossoms,
Herald the advent of Spring,
As Nature smiles wordlessly.

185. The blue from the sky,
Lends it's colour to the sea,
How close heaven and earth.

186. Prayer , the most powerful
Antidote to bouts of pain,
Like dew drops, like rain.

187. Bananas the fruit
That can drive you all crazy
Don't go bananas

188. Snows melt to rivers form
That twist and turn endlessly
In search of eternity

189. Think, touch , hear, see, smell,
Those that only with eyes see,
Miss the world's beauty.

190. Winds change direction
Treasure the moments of joy
You never know when.

191. You are your best friend
Be alone but not aloof,
Solitude is peace,

192. An eagle in flight
Soaring over distant clouds,
What a glorious sight.

193. Much like rivulets
Tears are meant to flow and dry
The cycle goes on,

194. Some puzzles aren't solved
The world is a conundrum
Life is mystery.

195. I gaze at the stars
As the moon shines down on me
The night is heavenly.

196. He uses his phone
To catch a moment's feeling
A high tech guru.

197. I heard a bird sing
The voice was heavenly
Was it an angel

198. The tree gives us shade
Why don't we treat it kindly
I wonder sometimes

199. Tigers and rhinos
Live together happily
Then why shouldn't Man?

200. A beautiful smile
Like a beautiful flower
Always nice to see.

201. Secrets that you keep
Well concealed within your heart,
The eyes will reveal.

202. Sweep cobweb's away
Cos they will clutter the mind
And then entrap you.

203. Nights are meant for sleep
And dreams to keep hopes alive,
Castles in the air.

204. Tranquility lies
In the shrines within the heart,
Not in stone temples.

205. Green leaves, Brown leaves all,
Oak trees, Elm trees, Fir trees all
Nature is supreme.

206. I wish I could fly
Somewhere miles into the sky
Soar and dream and soar.

207. Don't ask the gardener
Which flower is the prettiest,
No mother will choose.

208. Deep down in the heart
Every adult is a child
Every tree a seed .

209. Storms know and winds too
You can bend a reed but then
The reed will stand tall.

210. When I touch a leaf
With nature I am complete,
What more do I need!

211. Reminded I am,
When a drooping flower I see,
Of life's vagaries.

212. The Sun, the Moon, the stars,
Heavenly bodies all,
For me light and warmth.

213. The stars I can't touch,
And mountains I cannot climb,
Insignificance.

214. I see the tree breathe
And the quivering of its leaves
Then I feel alive.

215. The lines on the brow
Are the signs of troubled times,
Turmoil in the mind.

216. Drops of dew then rain
A freshness and then some pain
The heavens too will cry.

217. Time stands still for me
When the birds I see drifting
Aimlessly above.

218. Pretty daffodil
Your curves give me a thrill
Hope you're happy too.

219. "Take my power and pelf
And within me peace instill,"
Say most men to God.

220. Give me time and ear
Nothing else is yours, my dear
Even flowers are dust.

221. When sleep overtakes me
Why's there turmoil in the mind?
Is dawn uncertain?

222. The romantic Moon
Lonely without the Sun's gaze
Reflected glory.

223. Silence is serene
Serenity holds desire
Like embers, fire.

224. The tears from my eyes
Will a river form my friend
For you to float on.

225. To speak with a flower,
Needs a heart, the eyes won't do,
Unspoken caring.

226. The earth's aroma
No perfume will ever match,
O merciful rain.

227. A parrot, a crow
A vulture, eagle or kite,
Fly together, why can't man?

228. The cycle of life,
Eternal is balderdash,
All things have an end.

229. An eye for an eye,
As you sow so shall you reap,
Action, reaction.

230. Happiness spreads,
A smile will a smile return,
Warmth is contagious.

231. Blossom time long gone
Withered leaves their story tell
Is time a sadist?

232. Desert storms, earthquakes,
The harshness of nature,
Man will never learn.

233. Small things matter,
A little wave a storm makes,
And prayer restores calm.

234. How harmonious,
Ten thousand leaves on a tree,
Strength in unity.

235. The sun melts the snow
Melting snow a river makes
That nurtures all life.

236. Humble is supreme
Look at the stars in the sky
How bright, yet so small.

237. Not birds but like them
Butterflies are beautiful
Flying to and fro.

238. Green grass and fresh dew
Nature at it's very best
Bountifully true.

239. Taken for granted
The Sun, the stars and the Moon
How thankless is man?

240. The clouds are a veil
The silver lining the eyes
Beautiful Moon.

241. Typhoons devastate
Waves delight the shore no end
Little things are best.

242. Don't look for reasons
Some things are just meant to be,
Acceptance is wise.

243. Branches of a tree
Receive nourishment from roots
Man from ancestors.

244. Visions of the Lord
Now lie within stony hearts
How changed is our world.

245. Rainbows in the sky
Colours of the setting sun
Nature's gifts to man.

246. The stillness of trees
Brings happiness to the heart
Calm is truly bliss.

247. The beating heart is
So much like the ticking clock
Both keep track of time.

248. Separation hurts
Falling leaves make the tree weep
Bonding is true love.

249. When you shake a hand
Friendship is only the start
Learn to listen first.

250. Square pegs in round holes
Misfits are found everywhere
Unfortunately.

251. Learn from the tortoise
Slow and steady wins the race
Life, a marathon.

252. When you climb a hill
Remember the way down too
Heights take their toll, friend.

253. Think before you speak
A wild tongue can endanger
Like a loose cannon.

254. The Sun sustains all
The absence of light is night
Two sides of the coin.

255. Who knows what is next?
Must make hay while the sun shines
Opportunity.

256. The mind is fertile
Sow the field with truth and grace,
Harvest, calm and peace.

257. What is life, except
The elements in order?
Disarray is death.

258. Beautiful childhood
Catching tadpoles in the stream
Lovely memories.

259. Vengeance is futile
The day of reckoning looms
Beware, you seekers.

260. Passions drive us all
Unchained and unleashed like a
Tiger on the prowl.

261. An angioplasty keeps blood flowing
Through the veins
The heart's response good.

262. The warmth of closeness
No blanket can ever match
The natural touch.

263. When the Sun dips low
O, beautiful Moon you are
Reflected glory.

264. The whispering breeze
Through the willows makes its way
To my ears, then heart.

265. My oarsman is God
No seas will ever drown me
When faith is secure.

266. The rain's a blessing
There's no need for umbrellas
All sins get washed.

267. Write your words in stone
The tongue is a great twister
The friend of all lies.

268. How bright are the eyes
When the soul inside does glow?
All darkness dispelled.

269. All ants are workers
But all workers aren't ants
O, silly logic.

270. Typhoons, tsunamis
Earthquakes are nature's revenge
Will man never learn?

271. They fly nearest God,
Are birds the purest of all
His many creatures?

272. Flames set hearts alight
And flames keep the nights at bay
O, beautiful flames.

273 Haikus must make sense
In three lines a complete tale
And a story told.

274. Just three lines won't do
The structure is important
Homes are not mere doors.

275. Petals and the stem
As much a part of the rose
As is its perfume.

276. Big fish eats small fish
And the sea swallows the shark
We can't fight nature.

277. Love for walls and roofs
Love too for doors and windows
Love for place called home.

278. Tears are love and pain,
Thunder, lightning, gentle rain,
The nature of tears.

279. A sigh is remorse,
A sigh is contentment too,
A sigh is relief.

280. They're big and small too
Purring gently, roaring too,
Cats in the jungle.

281. Bliss is when I am alone
With time to atone,
For my transgressions.

282. Sighs are not just sighs
A tear is not just a drop
The heart has feelings.

283. Don't go by colours
Green is not always verdant
It is envy too.

284 Light and dark, two sides,
Blue is not always the sky
It is sombre too.

285. Indigo means sad
A purple patch is good luck
Colours are funny.

286. Learn humility,
From the drooping boughs of trees,
They give shade also.

ND - #0264 - 080726 - C0 - 197/132/7 - PB - 9781784562403 - Gloss Lamination